# DOG BREEDS

# Beagles

by Sara Green

Consultant:
Michael Leuthner, D.V.M.
PetCare Clinic, Madison, Wisc.

BLASTOFF! READERS 4

BELLWETHER MEDIA • MINNEAPOLIS, MN

**3 1561 00238 7201**

Note to Librarians, Teachers, and Parents:

**Blastoff! Readers** are carefully developed by literacy experts and combine standards-based content with developmentally appropriate text.

**Level 1** provides the most support through repetition of high-frequency words, light text, predictable sentence patterns, and strong visual support.

**Level 2** offers early readers a bit more challenge through varied simple sentences, increased text load, and less repetition of high-frequency words.

**Level 3** advances early-fluent readers toward fluency through increased text and concept load, less reliance on visuals, longer sentences, and more literary language.

**Level 4** builds reading stamina by providing more text per page, increased use of punctuation, greater variation in sentence patterns, and increasingly challenging vocabulary.

**Level 5** encourages children to move from "learning to read" to "reading to learn" by providing even more text, varied writing styles, and less familiar topics.

Whichever book is right for your reader, Blastoff! Readers are the perfect books to build confidence and encourage a love of reading that will last a lifetime!

This edition first published in 2009 by Bellwether Media.

Library of Congress Cataloging-in-Publication Data

Green, Sara, 1964-
  Beagles / by Sara Green.
    p. cm. — (Blastoff! readers. Dog breeds)
  Includes bibliographical references and index.
  Summary: "Simple text and full color photographs introduce beginning readers to the characteristics of Beagles. Developed by literacy experts for students in kindergarten through third grade"—Provided by publisher.
  ISBN-13: 978-1-60014-217-8 (hardcover : alk. paper)
  ISBN-10: 1-60014-217-6 (hardcover : alk. paper)
  1. Beagle (Dog breed)—Juvenile literature. I. Title.

SF429.B3G74 2008
636.753'7—dc22                                    2008019992

# Contents

Beagles are friendly dogs with floppy ears. They belong to a group of dogs called **scent hounds**. Beagles can smell many things that people cannot smell. They use their excellent sense of smell to learn about the world and do important work.

Beagles are small to medium-sized dogs that weigh 20 to 25 pounds (9 to 11 kilograms). They are 10 to 15 inches tall (30 to 38 centimeters).

Beagles have short, thick **coats**. Beagle coats are often black, white, and brown. This is called **tricolor**. Some Beagles have coats with just two colors.

# History of Beagles

No one knows exactly how the Beagle **breed** began. **Hunting dogs** called Talbot Hounds were probably the **ancestors** of Beagles. Talbot Hounds lived in England about 1000 years ago. They were mostly white. Talbot Hounds had puppies with other black and brown dogs. Their puppies were probably the first Beagles. Talbot Hounds are now **extinct**.

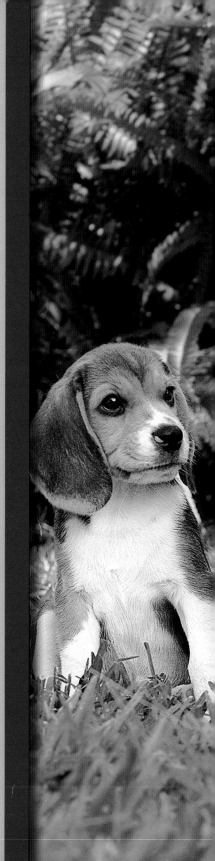

King Henry VIII was the King of England in the early 1500s. He owned many Beagles. Some were so small that they could fit in a pocket. These small Beagles were called Pocket Beagles.

Beagles were popular hunting dogs for people in England. They hunted hares and other small animals. These animals can move very fast. They can be very hard to see in tall grass or forests. Beagles were able to **track** the scent of these animals.

## fun fact

Pocket Beagles were also called Glove Beagles because they were so small they could fit in the palm of your hand. Pocket Beagles are rare today.

Beagles hunted in **packs**. Hunters followed the Beagles on foot. This type of hunting was called **beagling**.

By the 1700s, beagling became less popular. People bred fewer Beagles. Beagles almost became extinct. Fortunately, some farmers held onto their Beagles.

In the 1800s, people brought Beagles to the United States to hunt small animals. Beagles soon became popular house pets.

# Beagles Today

Beagles like to be with people or other dogs. Sometimes Beagles **bay** when they are left alone. The name Beagle may come from a French word that describes how Beagles open their mouths when they bay.

Outside, there are many smells for Beagles to explore. Beagles love to follow **scent trails**. A Beagle can wander for miles following a scent trail.

Beagles can use their sense of smell to help people. Some Beagles work in airports in the United States. They belong to the Beagle Brigade. These Beagles sniff for food in suitcases and packages.

Some food from other countries is not allowed in the United States because it might contain harmful insects or diseases. Beagles alert people when they smell these foods.

**fun fact**

In 2004, there were more than 60 Beagle Brigade teams at 21 airports in the United States.

Beagles are more than just working
dogs. They are still popular pets.

They are friendly dogs that use their sharp sense of smell to explore the world.

# Glossary

**ancestor**—a family member who lived long ago

**bay**—a deep howl

**beagling**—a type of hunting where people followed Beagles on foot to find animals

**breed**—a type of dog

**coat**—the hair or fur of an animal

**extinct**—when every member of a species has died off

**hunting dog**—a dog used by people to catch animals for food or sport

**pack**—a group of dogs

**scent hound**—a dog that uses its sense of smell to locate things

**scent trails**—smells animals or people leave behind as they travel

**track**—to follow an animal's trail

**tricolor**—having three colors; most Beagle coats have three colors.

# To Learn More

**AT THE LIBRARY**
Kallen, Stuart A. *Beagles*. Edina, Minn.:
Checkerboard Books, 1998.

Mulvany, Martha. *The Story of the Beagle*.
New York: Powerkids Press, 2000.

Stone, Lynn M. *Beagles*. Vero Beach, Fla.:
Rourke, 2002.

**ON THE WEB**
Learning more about Beagles
is as easy as 1, 2, 3.

1. Go to www.factsurfer.com

2. Enter "Beagles" into search box.

3. Click the "Surf" button and you will see a list of
   related web sites.

With factsurfer.com, finding more information is just a
click away.

# Index

The images in this book are reproduced through the courtesy of: Eric Isselee, front cover;
Mark Raycroft / Getty Images, pp. 4-5, 6, 7, 15; Tim Graham / Getty Images, p. 9;
Hans Holbein the Younger / Getty Images, p. 10; Hilarie Kavanagh / Getty Images, p. 11;
Photofusion Picture Library / Alamy, pp. 12-13; Pix 'n Pages, pp. 14, 17, 21; Getty Images, pp. 18-19;
John Cancalosi / agefotostock, p. 20.